MATTER

MATTER

·POEMS·

DAN BROWN

Crosstown Books
New York

© 1996 by Dan Brown
All rights reserved
Published by Crosstown Books
P.O. Box 1824
Cathedral Station
New York, NY 10025
Set in Baskerville by Sans Serif, Inc., Ann Arbor, MI
Printed by Thomson-Shore, Dexter, MI
Cover design: Jonathan Bumas
Cover art: detail from Peter McCulloch's "Cruachan" fabric,
provided courtesy of the Philadelphia Museum of Art;
gift of Hull Traders Ltd.

Cataloging in Publication Data

Brown, Dan, 1950–
Matter / Dan Brown.
p. cm.
ISBN 0–9647581–0–5 (hardcover)
ISBN 0–9647581–1–3 (paper)
I. Title.
PS3552.R69M38   1996
811'.54   95–090583   CIP

Acknowledgments

The author and publisher gratefully acknowledge the following publications in which these poems, sometimes in earlier versions, first appeared:

Cream City Review. "Where I Was"
The Formalist. "Epitaph for Deconstruction"
Partisan Review. "In the Chapel in My Head"
Poet and Critic. "A Wreck"
Poetry Northwest. "Approached at a Hotdog Stand"
Tar River Poetry. "Facing It"

"A Little Number" first appeared in *The Literature of Work: Short Stories, Essays, and Poems by Men and Women of Business* (Phoenix University Press). Part 2 of "Two Jobs for Ockham's Razor" appeared in *The Writing Path 1: An Annual of Poetry and Prose from Writers' Conferences* (University of Iowa Press).

The author would also like to thank Ray Bacon and Marie Merkel for their close editorial attention.

For Alice

Contents

Notice   3

Missing It   5
Something Like That   6
Where I Was   7
In the Chapel in My Head   9
My Own Traces   10
Why I'm Not an Aesthetician   11
On Being Asked by Our Receptionist if I Liked
    the Flowers   12
Approached at a Hotdog Stand   13
The Wind   15
Two Jobs for Ockham's Razor   16
The Olden Times   19
A New York View   20
Since He Asked   21
A Little Number   22
Facing It   23

Report   27

An Aspect of Having Her   29
Epitaph for Deconstruction   30
Score One   31
Well Up in the Blessings   33
Arnie   34
Taking the Occasion   35
Epiphany   36
A Salmon Speaks   37
Judo   39
The Birth of God   40
Prayer   42

A Wreck   43

Deliverance   47

Valédiction   49

Author's Note   51

MATTER

Notice

Indolent I wouldn't know because
I never was that, forget how
It ever looked. What I was was getting
Ready, and the getting's over now.

Missing It

The thing about the old one about
The tree in the forest and nobody's around
And how it falls maybe with a sound,
Maybe not, is you throw the part out
About what there isn't or there is,
And the part of it that haunts is still there.
Still there in that the happening, the clear
Crashing there, still encompasses
Everyone condemned to missing it
By being out of the immediate
Vicinity. Out of it the way
You're out of all vicinities but one
All the time. Till presently you've gone
Out of all vicinities to stay.

Something Like That

You know how in Spanish they put
An -ita on things? So this girl
Mildred, this Puerto Rican girl
Where I work, pretty girl—so I get
To thinking that a funny thing about
Her name is that it's one thing that now
That you think of it it isn't clear how
To ita-ize.
           I'd ask her straight out,
But something tells me it would be a bit
Better to let the questioning begin
With something in the way of easing in.
As in it is Spanish isn't it
Where they do that, and are we talking small
Things specifically or is it more
Like anything you have affection for
And so forth and so on . . . All
Of which preliminary inquiries
Get me to the one I'm getting at:
Did they ever call her something like that
When she was a kid?
                  Only lowered eyes.
Then, like something she's confessing to,
That her father did. And would she mind my
Asking what it was? No reply,
So I try a little prompting with a few
Possibilities. Not to press her,
But I've got to know how that would go:
Mildrita? "No." Mildredita? "No."
Mildredecita? "No!" Then . . . "Princesa."

Where I Was

I was in Princeton of all
Places. My ninth grade class
Was there on a field trip: the usual
Shepherding from edifice
To edifice—a lot of gray
Stone—winding up, though,
With something a little out of the way:
The opportunity to view
A classic three-acter
At the U's own theater.

The play I don't remember much
About: your basic exercise
In wigs and bodices and such.
The memorable thing was
The curtain call. How the one
Coming out was a grim guy
In tweed and tie. How the lone
Lifting of his palm by
Itself extinguished the applause.
How he had "terrible news"—

But not the news I feared. Not
Where to go. Not how
To get there. Not what
To do when you got there—go
Sit against the wall, put
Your head down, clasp your hands
Behind your head, you might shut
Your eyes in case the world ends—
None of that. Maybe he
Was finding it decidedly

7

Hard to get the words out,
But what the words amounted to
Wasn't the worst thing: not
Anything that had to do
With going up in a cloud of hell,
But rather with the President,
A motorcade, a hospital—
With how the evident extent
Of anybody's sudden death
Was elsewhere and over with.

In the Chapel in My Head

Having gone
an especially rough round
on the phone with her,
I repaired to the chapel in my head.

Onto whose pew
I'd no sooner settled
than the Lord boiled up by the altar and boomed
"I gave you a tongue.
Abuse it
and I'll pluck it out."

"Hasten the day," I said.

My Own Traces

Dish sinked, food stowed—
So maybe I should hit the road.
A yank at the cord of what

I'd call the kitchen light if this
Nook were more of an excuse
For calling it that.

Whereupon the making for
The freedom of the front door—
In the course of which is when

The awful certainty of my
Never sealing up the rye
Bread steals in.

Nothing but to turn around,
Back-track to where I find
Myself re-entering

The province of the kitchenette,
Only to confront the sight
Of the light-cord aswing.

Not the first case of my
Own traces taking me
Completely by surprise.

Moving me to mutter "So
I *do* exist"—much as though
I'd had it otherwise.

Why I'm Not an Aesthetician

Here's to the tunes
With the brains to hit
Their highest note
Only once,

And the every bit
As brilliant ones
That have the sense
To hammer it.

On Being Asked by Our Receptionist
if I Liked the Flowers

"What flowers?" I said. "These flowers," she said,
Gesturing leftward with her head,
And there it was: a vase of flowers
That hadn't graced that fort of hers
The day before. Did I say a vase?
All of an urn is what it was:
Capacious home to a bursting sun
Of thirty lilies if to one.
A splendor I'd have seen for sure—
If less employed in seeing her.

Approached at a Hotdog Stand

Don't ask me how but somehow
I know I'm about to have to hear
Something that I don't *want* to have
To hear: "Psst, pal, 's it O.K.
We talk for a minute? How about
You look at this nice radio.

Pretty nice little radio,
Huh pal?" Just tell me how
Come he gets to say how about
Anything, particularly here
Where whether or not I think it's O.K.
Makes no difference if I have

To stand here the way I *do* have
To. I don't need a radio,
I tell him. "'Cause your basic O.K.
Radio is one thing but how
About when it makes what you hear
Sound like this? Or what about

This, huh? Or whadya think about
This, huh pal? Plus you have . . .
Just let me tune it in here . . . "
But I already have a radio,
I tell him. " . . . just let . . . Anyhow
They all come in O.K.

Almost always, O.K.?
Sure I'm not that sure about
In the subway, say—but then how
Often are you really gonna have

13

To listen to the damn radio
Down there where who's gonna hear

Anything anyway . . . Hear
That? That's the Yankees, O.K.?
See why you want a radio?
The Yankees that's what it's about.
The Yankees that's why you gotta *have*
A radio; your radio's how

You *hear* those Yankees, hey how
About those Yankees—so you have
A radio already O.K."

The Wind

It doesn't know
the plains from the sea:
two chances
to be given its head.
What it kicks up—
the waves that sweep the wheat,
the roving cliffs of water—
it never looks back at.
Should it meet
with a mast, a steeple, a tree,
nothing untoward transpires:
what it can't topple
it passes.
When it moans
it's just us.

Two Jobs for Ockham's Razor

1.

Of an evening *en café,*
A certain girl at the display-
Counter. Not the girl as
Such as much as how she's
Rendering herself. The way
She's pressing up against the display-
Glass. The way the pressing has
Of rendering the girl's haunches.

Only later, when I stood
Up at the same counter, did
I find myself aware of how
The glass slanted in. How
The slanting-in-ness of it made
The glass a glass that *anybody'd*
Press against. The kind you
Fell on into.

2.

From the history of 5th (right
In front of the Library): They
Hadn't taken the grandstand
Down from some Day the day

Before. What was funny was
The extent to which the thing was still
Occupied—as though its mere
Presence made it capable

Of peopling itself. There
Were as many as fifty or so of us
At any rate, all taking
In the scene, such as

It was: not yesterday's
Respectable parade; just
The usual unruly one.
A good fifty or so, most

Of whom presumably had paused,
In the course of a busy afternoon,
To clamber up and settle down
And wave it all serenely on.

I liked that. Liked how,
Given a nice place to sit,
A body of souls was sitting there,
Whatever obligations not

Withstanding. Not that I had
A lot to do, but it looked as though
Enough of the others probably did:
Suits and white shirts and so

Forth. And yet what they
Amounted to was nothing less
Than a village of the idle in
A city of the sedulous.

Sure, it shook my view a bit
When half the villagers or more
Went storming down as one upon
The pulling up of an M-4

Bus. But there was the other half.
The half that happened to survive.
The half that lasted all the way
To the pulling up of an M-5.

The Olden Times

Hardly an especially
Sensitive futurion,
But get him thinking back upon
The olden times when people had
To die and *knew* they had to die—
You're looking at a shaking head.

A New York View

Word from Valley Spring:
Yet another loss
To the jury duty thing.
In this case our boss—
And this time for all
Of a six weeks' haul.

Discussion on the floor—
Where a gal and I get
To interchanging our
Guesses as to what
Manner of affair
Is doing up there.

My guess? A murder trial.
(Presumably a doing
That takes a little while.)
She: "In Valley Spring?
Murder? Never murder.
Maybe attempted murder."

Since He Asked

O what am I that I should not seem
For the song's sake a fool?

Yeats

Not to *say* what, but that strain
Of his that seems the singing of a loon:
Were it capable of helping us to bear
Reality's considerable weight—
To say this much is to despair
Of ever asking it to do that.

I grant you he could be more wrong
With reference to imperishable song.
Grant you that the fashioning of such
Is often done, even *only* done,
At fever pitch—and yet a fever pitch
Of reason if the truth be known.

A Little Number

"A guy comes swinging in the door
Looking for a feature for
His Model 2. Me being me,
I take the opportunity
To do a little number on
The Model 3. Expound upon
The many wonders of it. How
It's lighter. How the letters glow
Brighter. How it does ten,
Even twenty times again
As many things . . .
                              "He clearly buys
The better part of this—but says
He's worried that the 3 is more
Computer than he's ready for.
After all, a wizard you
Couldn't call him on the 2.
I smile—and proceed to play
The card that puts the guy away.
Namely—and you're gonna love
This—that that's the beauty of
The Model 3. A model so
Potent that your basic no-
Wizard on a 3 can do
What *takes* a wizard on a 2."

Facing It

I rarely think of genius of
The math variety without
Finding myself thinking about
An episode you gotta love.

It happened back in college. I
Was crossing the quad early one
Evening—maybe no sun
Any more, but still a sky

To speak of, if not to go
On about: the ritual
Indigo of nightfall—
Crossing, as I say, when who

Do I pick up approaching on
An intersect course but one
Eigenmeyer; just the one
Example of a math gēn'

At the place, so I'd been
Creditably told. A guy
I maybe knew to say Hi
To. Not a friend of mine

Or anything . . . So here it is:
A chance for us to reaffirm
This state of affairs for the fall term.
Each of us emitting his

"Hi." At least one of us
Wondering exactly what
There was to do beyond that,
When—listen! Are we hearing geese?

The sound is barely there—but that's
All it takes to get the eye
Directed at the north sky . . .
A hundred plus, we're looking at.

Obvious believers in
The 'V'-ness of getting there,
Relative to going air-
Wise. All coming on

Towards us deliverèd
Ones. *Damn* clamorous
In passing on over us—
Whence the 'V' of them proceed

To propagate a sorrow not
Quite another sorrow is,
In passing on away . . . And as
For Eigenmeyer: And as for what

If anything there was to say
To such a one at such a time—
Perhaps you'll pardon me if I'm
Proud of how my digging way

Down enabled me to come
Up with something apropos:
To wit, did Eigenmeyer know
That somehow or other some

Sort of bird or other'd been
Shown to count as high as eight?
He answers that he would have thought
Nine. I ask him why nine.

He says I wouldn't understand:
With nothing you could call conceit,
Nothing you could call regret.
Tell me I'm supposed to mind.

Report

Things have gotten far
Enough along to where
I actually see
Myself getting there.

An Aspect of Having Her

Maybe having Alice hasn't
Bettered *everything*—but then,
Aseat on a babe-bedotted bus,
I open to some scandal in

A *Daily News* I'd picked up
(Being in a *News* mood)—
Only to experience
The wonted glow of gratitude

For one of the many gifts that *have*
Come with having her: the not
Having to worry lest some
Times-type rule me out.

Epitaph for Deconstruction

A puff of wind that really shouldn't
Have blown so many so far astray—
And yet not anyone who wouldn't
Have come to nothing anyway.

Score One

Saying that you just can't win—
That's not to say you *never* can.
Take what happened one day
In a class I was giving. This was back
When I was visiting in music
At a college that it's fairly safe to say
You wouldn't have heard of. So I'm up
In front of this Music 1-type
Class—big class, being held
In a big amphitheater-type hall—
Up there giving them the deal
On rhythm. Meaning getting them sold
On just how significant a thing
It really is. At any rate trying.

There was this little exercise
I used to work in here: tap
Out a rhythm with a pen-top
And see if anyone can recognize
What song it is from just that.
Which everybody's pretty good at
Given that you use the right song.
"For He's a Jolly Good Fellow's" a good one—
Among another fifty million.
Though that many more are all wrong:
"The Flight of the Bumblebee," for instance—
Though somebody might have a chance
If you let it go on long enough . . .
The which would take two hands and two
Pens if you were really gonna do
It. . . . Anyway, I start off
As usual, with the selfsame glee

Above adduced—which they identify
Right off, of course. Follow up
With a couple more near as easy ones
By way of building up their confidence—
And find myself looking at a group
That whether or not they're tuned in to what
All this is even getting at
They're soaring on the wings of a new
Mastery—itself an unsmall
Thing, yes?
                    At which point in all
Of which a hand undertakes to go
Up: a kid wondering if I
Would mind if he tried one on *me*.
One, furthermore, that while I should
Know he doesn't think I *do* know.

Should know but don't know: now
That could be what? "Go ahead,"
I tell him. "Let's hear what you've got"—
And slip my pen back into my pocket
And stand there waiting. Whereupon
He starts clapping out some hymn
Kind of thing or march thing or some-
Thing. Little else to go on—
Beyond what *he* has to go
On in not expecting me to know.
Also not a lot if you consider.
There's the bare fact of my position . . .
The fact that it's a visiting position. . . .

No sooner do I utter "alma mater"
Than everybody's standing up as one . . .
Breathing in as one . . . launching in.

Well Up In the Blessings

Well up in the blessings there's
The blessedness of knowing
That vision, skin, body, brain
Have all started going.

For how it is with death is how
It is with anything:
Easier to accept when it's
Already happening.

Arnie

Some reasoning of which he once
Delivered himself was in response
To an awful break: golf ball
Snugged into a gopher hole;
Fully a hundred yards still
To go. Whence the usual
Obtrusion of a microphone—
Eliciting in turn the un-
Varnished voice of the champion.
That yes, the ball was sitting down
A little bit—but at least he
Could see it. And what he could see he
Could hit. And what he could hit he
Could move. And what he could move he
Could sink. Not get toward the green
Or on the green or near the pin
(Imaginable feats, if none
You'd want to bet your pension on)
But sink. Sink! Completely mad,
If very nearly what he did.

Taking the Occasion

Among the memories I love?
Your taking the occasion of
A walk across the kitchen floor
To lift into tiptoe
And pirouette: a *prima* mo-
Mentarily forevermore.

Epiphany

At moments it can seem as though
The thoughts I'm thinking in
Aren't just a case of being
No thoughts of mine
But no thoughts at all—not
If intellect implies
Something less suggestive of
A tripping of relays.

It's one thing to entertain
A notion of the self
As a chimera constructed from
Components off the shelf;
Another thing entirely
To have the truth of this
As present to the sentience as
Your hand before your face.

Granted this epiphany,
I'm not inclined to blame
The vision when it dissipates
As quickly as it came.
Nor to blame myself for seeing
Nothing to deplore
In the matter of its not having
Changed things more.

A Salmon Speaks

You approach it
with an image of it
but nothing prepares you for it.

You don't even know
you've reached it at first:
that strange taste could mean anything.
You keep to your heading,
the riversilt clears . . .

Lucent in its upper reaches,
a vast domain dims in descent,
gradually devolving toward a blackness
one fins through life
trying not to think about.

Yet up from that nethernight
jut those peaks and ridges
which provide so much of the grandeur here.
Much of the interest too,
their faces being
very carnivals of incident.
Especially compelling
are those dramas
it's healthier to witness than to live.
How some of them stay with me!
Like that silverlittle's despondent swim
right down the throat of an anemone:
as though loveloss
had crushed it past caring.
Never more finally
has a clutch of white worms

closed over its hole.
And yet . . .
the giant fans,
their fronds asway
in the waterwind . . .
the manta ray,
its glide a thing
of a ripple of wing . . .
the jellyfish,
that inside out
heart of light . . .
in singing these sublimities
I ask the several
to stand for the innumerable.

Such richesse!
The river was nice,
but never like this.
I have no intention
of ever getting over it.

Judo

I.e., the kind of verse
That doesn't try to force
People to their knees
(Seeing as it sees
To people's being thrown
By moment of their own).

The Birth of God

It happened near Lascaux
A million dawns ago.
For dawn it was,
Infusing radiance
And cuing avians
The way it does,

That saw the two of them
(I see a her and him,
But maybe not)
Emerging from the mouth
Of a cave a couple south
Of the one that's got

All that painted fauna
All but snorting on a
Wall. That is
To say, from the mouth of a cave
Unconsecrated save
By the sighs and cries

Of the night just past. The pair
Has borne the bliss they share
Out into the bright.
Where silently they stand
Thanking, hand in hand
Before the light.

Their gratitude is truly
New beneath the duly
Erupting sun.
A gratitude that so

Wants a place to go
It authors one.

Prayer

Repeatedly
A new house
Larger than
The previous—

In each case
The previous
Persisting as
A part of us—

This growth as
Of the nautilus
May our selves
Suffer us.

A Wreck

One of the signal incidents of my
Musicology days was a memory-
Slip I once heard in a concert.
Actually a wreck was more like it.
The player in this case was someone
I happened to know. A woman I'd first run

Across on the Arts quad—and may the heart
Forever unrecover from the hurt
It suffered at the first sight of her:
Seated in the shade of a great oak,
Reading—clearly somebody at
Whom I was gonna have to get

A closer look. The which I engineer
In terms of a go-by. And yes a dire
Beauty inheres there, but what's really
Clinching is the fact that what she's
Reading turns out to be music.
Given which I round my way back

To near where she's sitting, casually
Sit myself down close by,
Kill some time . . . then strike something up.
Turns out that she's a psych grad,
Bach notwithstanding—though she does
Dabble in piano. Which allows

The posing of a certain next step:
That how about the two of us slip
Off into a practice room and treat

Ourselves to a little bit of four-hand.
Which we do. And have such a good
Time doing it that we decide

Not to let that be that.
Meaning there's another such date,
Not to mention yet another one
And another one and so on—to the point
Where one day I wake up to find
Myself in a relation of a kind.

Understand about this relation:
I couldn't tell you just how it's done,
But she manages on the one hand to hold
Out the hopes of something serious . . .
Yet says without saying it that don't
Think that it'll happen, when it won't.

And doesn't. Which becomes a little old
After a while . . . Would render things cold
Totally, in time. But hadn't yet
When she's visited with the image of her giving
A no-kidding concert. And yes
(You wouldn't have caught *me* doing this)

Actually makes a fact of it.
Actually books an intimate
Little hall, posts some notices
(With her picture yet), and winds up in front
Of a none-too-shabby gathering.
Nor for that matter is her *playing*

Shabby. Fact is, she manages
Admirably. Does so, that is,
Until she breaks down altogether.
As for just exactly what happened—

First of all, it's not irrelevant
That it happened in a Schubert last movement;

One of those ones of his where
The main theme comes back over
And over; each time—and this did
The damage—each time leading in
To a new next thing of some kind.
So here she is, things well in hand

Apparently, just having played
The theme the third time (having played
The heart out of the damn thing to boot);
Beginning the third next thing—but no!
The one that's underway is the *fourth* one!
A little ways into which is when

It hits her that she's left something out.
Or seems to, given the upshot:
The pulling up short; the sitting there
For a bit. . . . Then an attempt to go on
Anyway. A hard thing to do
Once the thread's gone. Not so

Hard, though, that you'd expect the sheer-
Ness of the disintegration here:
Pieces of the piece surfacing
Like pieces of debris from a shipwreck.
I remember trading looks with someone;
Another guy a few seats down.

A guy, I find myself noticing,
With nobody with him. Strange thing,
In fact, the way a number of such guys
Are scattered-in here. In fact a good

Half the house, is what it looks like.
Of course there's the matter of the look

Of her, in particular of those
Dive-in eyes, God knows . . .
It's one thing, acknowledging the sway
Of beauty, but to see it in the guise
Of a veritable nation of the swayed . . .
Is only to affirm the brotherhood

Of those of us fated to convey
Beauty on its whither-which way,
Fate have mercy . . . In the mean-
Time she's picked up the thread again;
To the point of getting toward the end—as,
For our part, we ready the applause.

Deliverance

When I think about how
We deal with our mortality
I think about a sense in which it's like we
Deal with an injury.

About how, having
First happened upon the hurt-
Ness, we harrow it and harrow it:
This at the behest of that

Cave-old, even
Ocean-old imperative
To reckon at its maximally grave
Any injury we have.

How, years having passed,
We find ourselves doing it
But intermittently, and more by rote
Than necessity: our purpose not

To sound the wound so much as
To remind ourselves it's still there.
How one day we're suddenly aware
Of its no longer being there.

Valediction

Good, bad or what,
I've given it a shot.

Author's Note

As near as I can be objective about it (i.e., not in the least), I see the poems in this book as having something significant to offer. If you see them similarly, perhaps you'd be interested in helping them reach some additional readers.

Feel free, for example, to recommend *Matter* to a friend or two. To carry this approach a step further, if your local newspaper reviews books, why not recommend that it review this one? Write me care of my publisher Crosstown Books,* and I'll see that a copy of *Matter* is sent to any reviewer you suggest.

Beyond reviewers proper are journalists who cover the book beat (or the cultural scene in general). They tend to be as interested in the story behind a book as the book per se. As it happens, the story behind *Matter* is noteworthy. It's recounted in a press release available to anyone in the media you suggest (or to you yourself if you're interested). Again, write me care of Crosstown Books.

Did I mention that I give an unusual sort of poetry reading? It's actually a reading/lecture hybrid, in which I use poems by myself and others as a jumping-off point for a discussion of poetry and poetics in general. If you'd like to have this presentation in your locality, contact me via Crosstown.

I'm not entirely comfortable in making these suggestions (though more comfortable than you may be in reading them), but if an artist believes in his work, how can he be blamed for trying to bring it to the notice of as many people as possible? In discussing Robert Frost's notorious penchant for self-promotion, Joseph Brodsky once said, "If you'd written such poems, you'd promote them too." I honestly feel that I've written something not unlike such poems: poems which play a New Yorker's voice, as Frost's played a New Englander's, across the back-beat of meter and rhyme; poems which have substantial things to say and say them clearly. I'd kick myself forever if I didn't risk everything, your displeasure included, to help them do what good they can do in the world.

Dan Brown
New York, August, 1995

*Crosstown Books
P.O. Box 1824
Cathedral Station
New York, NY 10025

About the Author

Dan Brown was raised in and around New York City. Following early studies in composition and musicology at Cornell University, he switched to the computer field. He currently works for IBM in Manhattan.